10 CARING GOALS

JANE BURNARD • FATTI BURKE

PowerKiDS press.

Published in 2027
by The Rosen Publishing Group, Inc.
2544 Clinton Street, Buffalo, NY 14224

First published in Great Britain in 2022 by Wayland

Credits

Editor: Julia Bird
Editorial, design and project management: Raspberry Books
Design: Intrepid Books LTD
Illustrations: Fatti Burke

Cataloging-in-Publication Data

Names: Burnard, Jane, author. | Burke, Fatti, illustrator.
Title: 10 caring goals / written by Jane Burnard, illustrated by Fatti Burke.
Description: Buffalo, New York : PowerKids Press, 2027. | Series: 10 goals | Includes glossary and index.
Identifiers: ISBN 9781499459036 (pbk.) | ISBN 9781499459043 (library bound) | ISBN 9781499459050 (ebook)
Subjects: LCSH: Caring--Juvenile literature. | Self-care, Health--Juvenile literature.
Classification: LCC BJ1475 B876 2027 | DDC 177.7--dc23

Printed in China
CPSIA Compliance Information: Batch #QS27PK. For further information contact Rosen Publishing at 1-800-237-9932.

CONTENTS

Caring helps others and makes us FEEL Good!

WHY CARING GOALS ARE GOOD

What do you get if you mix together caring, kindness, compassion, empathy, and love?

All these add up to the same, wonderful thing - feeling warmth towards others and wanting to do something to help them or make them feel happy. When we care for other people, it doesn't only benefit them, it benefits us too, so the more you do for others, the bigger your own smile will be!

What's more, kindness can become a habit. The more that people are kind and caring, the more capacity they have for even more kindness.

Could the grown-ups you live with do with a kind word? Does your best friend need a hand with their homework? Maybe your dog would love you to play with him!

If you want to care more for **EVERYONE**, this is the best place to start. Step by step, these ten caring goals will help you develop caring habits and start spreading the love!

GOAL 1

CARING for YOURSELF

There's only one, wonderful YOU, and you deserve the very best of care. So this goal is all about making sure you look after yourself really well.

How kind are you to yourself? Do you look after your body and mind, keep yourself safe and well and do the things that make you feel useful and happy?

Getting regular exercise, eating good food, drinking plenty of water, keeping clean, brushing your teeth, and sleeping well make our bodies healthier and fitter.

ACTIVITIES WE ENJOY, SUCH AS LISTENING TO OUR FAVORITE MUSIC, READING A BOOK OR PLAYING FOOTBALL WITH FRIENDS, HELP US LOOK AFTER OUR MINDS AND RELAX.

Reminding ourselves of all our good points, like being kind to our friends, makes us feel confident and happy.

WHEN OUR MINDS AND OUR BODIES ARE IN GOOD SHAPE WE FEEL A GREAT SENSE OF ACHIEVEMENT, WHICH CAN BOOST OUR SELF-ESTEEM, TOO.

All in all, caring for ourselves makes us feel great. And when we feel great, we're much more able to give to others.

Now, let's begin. Start a brand-new notebook and call it your Caring Notebook. Then turn this page to find out what to do with it!

TOP TIPS FOR CARING FOR YOURSELF

Here are five great ways to make yourself as happy and healthy as possible.

Wow! Did you realize how fantastic you are?

1 DRAW A MIND MAP

Write your name in a circle and draw lines out from it, saying on each one why you're a good person and a good friend.

2 GET ACTIVE

DO ONE HOUR OF EXERCISE, LIKE SOCCER, CYCLING, OR WALKING, EVERY DAY. EXERCISE DEVELOPS MOVEMENT SKILLS, MUSCLES, AND BONES. IT'S FUN, TOO!

3 EAT AND DRINK HEALTHILY

Cut down on sugary snacks and drinks and eat more lovely fruit, vegetables, and protein-rich foods, such as nuts. A healthy diet and plenty of fresh water can help our brains work well and make us calmer and happier.

4 LIST WHAT YOU LOVE

WRITE DOWN THE THINGS THAT MAKE YOU FEEL HAPPY AND RELAXED – THIS MAY BE SPENDING TIME WITH YOUR FAMILY OR FRIENDS, READING A GOOD BOOK, OR PLAYING A SPORT. THEN DO MORE OF THEM!

5 GET PLENTY OF SLEEP

Sleep makes you happier, more alert and attentive, and better able to learn. Plus, it puts you in a good mood in the morning!

GOAL 2

DEVELOPING A CARING MIND

How do you feel when you're kind to someone? You probably feel good. Because when we're kind, or when someone is nice to us, we make a "kindness hormone" called oxytocin.

Oxytocin makes us feel happy and brings our stress levels down.

A caring friend is the best friend you can have.

So how can we become even kinder and happier? Here are two FOOLPROOF ways.

1. BY LEARNING THE SKILL OF EMPATHY! THIS MEANS UNDERSTANDING OR IMAGINING WHAT LIFE IS LIKE FOR OTHER PEOPLE AND HOW THEY ARE FEELING. IT BRINGS US CLOSER TO PEOPLE. ALL HUMANS ARE CAPABLE OF EMPATHY, BUT WE CAN ALL DEVELOP THIS SPECIAL SKILL EVEN FURTHER.

So, instead of being mad next time your friend snaps at you or is in a bad mood, show empathy. Put yourself in their shoes and try to understand their feelings. Ask them how they are and listen carefully to their answers. Then take positive action to help them, if you can.

2. By counting kindnesses. This means remembering the good actions we've taken for ourselves and others. Some of these actions might be things we did that no one else noticed. They still matter! Counting kindnesses gives us confidence and improves our self-esteem, making us even more able to give.

Now you're ready to take caring action!

TOP TIPS TO DEVELOP A CARING MIND

Here are some practical ways to develop a kind, caring mind.

1 SPEND MORE TIME LISTENING THAN TALKING

Listening and trying to understand people's feelings is the best way to empathize. Remember to look for other clues to how they're feeling, such as their facial expressions and tone of voice.

2 WATCH FILMS AND READ BOOKS

THESE HELP US FEEL AND UNDERSTAND OTHER PEOPLE'S EMOTIONS. TRY *THE BFG* BY ROALD DAHL, *THE BOY AT THE BACK OF THE CLASS* BY ONJALI Q. RAÚF, *ONCE* BY MORRIS GLEITZMAN, *ASHA AND THE SPIRIT BIRD* BY JASBINDER BILAN OR THE HARRY POTTER BOOKS OR FILMS. ACTING IN PLAYS HAS THE SAME EFFECT!

3 COUNT YOUR KINDNESSES

In your Caring Notebook, list all the kind things you do and all the people you've helped so far, even if it's something as simple as giving someone a smile. Write down how these actions make you feel.

4 GET INSPIRED

TAKE INSPIRATION FROM KIND, LOVING PEOPLE. THEY MAY HAVE LIVED LONG AGO, OR THEY MIGHT BE YOUR GRANNY OR YOUR TEACHER!

When we're kind and loving, we exercise the regions of the brain that deal with empathy, compassion and positive emotion. As we continue to be caring, these "kindness muscles" develop and grow, making us feel happier and more able to give.

We live with them. We know them better than anyone in the world.

But do we care for the people at home in the way they deserve?

GOAL 3

CARING FOR THE PEOPLE YOU LIVE WITH

Just because you live with someone doesn't mean you always know how they're feeling. Give everyone the gift of your **ATTENTION** by checking in with them and asking how they are. Try to listen to their answers without talking about yourself.

DOES YOUR LITTLE SISTER OR BROTHER ASK YOU TO PLAY WITH THEM, WHEN YOU'D RATHER BE DOING SOMETHING ELSE? MAKE THEM HAPPY BY PUTTING THEIR NEEDS FIRST AND DOING WHAT THEY WANT FOR A LITTLE WHILE.

Is your parent or carer always bothering you to clean your room? Give them the gift of your **RESPECT** by doing as they ask.

BEING CLOSE TO PEOPLE MEANS THERE WILL SOMETIMES BE DISAGREEMENTS AND ARGUMENTS. TAKE A DEEP BREATH AND GIVE THEM THE GIFT OF YOUR **APOLOGY** AND/OR **FORGIVENESS** AS SOON AS YOU CAN.

Caring gifts like these will help create a happy home!

TOP TIPS FOR CARING FOR THE PEOPLE YOU LIVE WITH

Did you know that kindness is contagious? When someone receives a kindness, they are more likely to be nice to someone else. So, one small kind act can spread and spread and spread ...

Here are more ideas for spreading kindness in your own home.

Think of one way to help each household member or make them feel happy. Then go ahead and do it.

1 HELP OUT

Grown-ups are often tired at the end of the day. Make life easier for them by helping out in the kitchen, or keeping your room clean, so they can relax for a while.

2 GIVE YOUR ATTENTION

REMEMBER, TO YOUNGER SISTERS AND BROTHERS YOU'RE A HERO! MAKE THEIR DAY BY DOING A PUZZLE WITH THEM OR READING THEM A BEDTIME STORY. PLAY GAMES WITH THEM. GIVE THEM A BIG HUG. THEY'LL LOVE IT!

3 BE KIND

Does your older brother look sad? Ask him what's wrong and how you can help. Put on his favorite music. Or invite him out for a walk, so he can talk about things.

Remember, everything starts at home, but we use the caring skills we develop there with people outside, too.

4 BE THOUGHTFUL

MAYBE YOUR BIG SISTER'S JUST PASSED AN IMPORTANT EXAM? SHARE HER HAPPINESS BY MAKING HER A HANDMADE CONGRATULATIONS CARD.

GOAL 4

CARING FOR FRIENDS

What would we do without our friends? We share so much with them – company, secrets, fun, and support. Friendship is a wonderful gift – and Goal 4 is all about giving it to as many people as we can.

A caring friend:

- Listens to you and remembers what you tell them. Then follows it up by asking how you are.
- Is there for you – even in tough times.
- UNDERSTANDS YOUR LIKES AND DISLIKES.
- Shares their thoughts, feelings, and belongings with you.
- Is not jealous.
- FORGIVES YOU WHEN YOU MAKE MISTAKES.
- Encourages you to have other friends, too.
- Is honest, without being hurtful.
- LAUGHS WITH YOU.
- Is glad for your successes, and wishes your pain away.

WITH ALL YOUR FRIENDS, ALWAYS BE ON THE LOOKOUT FOR WAYS TO HELP THEM AND MAKE THEM HAPPY.

And remember, no one's perfect! You and your friends are going to disagree sometimes. When you do, make up as soon as you can – admit your faults, forgive them for theirs, then put it all behind you. See page 39 for more on this. Friendship is too precious to lose!

TOP TIPS FOR CARING FOR FRIENDS

Caring for our friends makes them happy, and it strengthens important friendship bonds.

Think of one good way to help a friend or make them happy.

For example:

BE THEIR STUDY BUDDY AND GIVE THEM POSITIVE FEEDBACK ON THEIR WORK.

Celebrate their achievements and special occasions – homemade cards and presents are great because they show we've taken time and thought.

Tell them how great their new haircut looks. (But if they're not happy with it, sympathize and tell them it'll quickly grow out!) Play their favorite sport or game. Tell them a joke!

And if they're feeling down:

USE YOUR BEST LISTENING SKILLS TO UNDERSTAND THEIR FEELINGS AND EMPATHIZE.

Suggest going for a walk and a chat.

INVITE THEM OVER TO WATCH THEIR FAVORITE FILM.

Lend them your favorite top (the one they've admired for ages).

Make new friends!

THE WORLD IS FULL OF POTENTIAL NEW FRIENDS. PERHAPS YOU HAVE A NEW CLASSMATE? GIVE THEM A FRIENDLY SMILE AND INTRODUCE THEM TO YOUR FRIENDS. INVITE THEM TO JOIN IN YOUR ACTIVITIES AND SIT NEXT TO THEM AT LUNCHTIME. YOU'VE JUST GAINED A GREAT NEW FRIEND!

Keep on caring for your friends and keep thinking of new ways to care.

GOAL

5

CARING FOR OLDER PEOPLE

Are you lucky enough to have older relatives or friends? Grandparents, great grandparents, great aunts and uncles? Then you'll know that older people deserve the **Greatest of care.**

Here are some of the Great things about older people:

They (usually!) love the company of young people.

THEY CAN TELL US ABOUT THE PAST.

THEY KEEP FAMILY STORIES AND HISTORY ALIVE, STRENGTHENING FAMILY AND COMMUNITY BONDS.

They've had lots of amazing life experience.

THEY TEND TO BE GOOD PROBLEM-SOLVERS.

THEY'RE NOT USUALLY IN A BIG RUSH, UNLIKE LOTS OF OTHER ADULTS.

MOST OF THEM WANT TO LIVE A PURPOSEFUL AND HELPFUL LIFE.

Life's not always easy for older people, though. Perhaps their life-partner has died, leaving them on their own. Maybe they've lost other friends and family, too. They might be suffering from illnesses that affect their hearing, sight, or ability to walk. All these are very good reasons for us to care for them.

IF YOU DON'T HAVE OLDER RELATIVES WHO LIVE NEAR YOU, ASK YOUR PARENT OR CARER IF YOU CAN HELP THEM LOOK AFTER AN ELDERLY NEIGHBOR. TOGETHER, YOU COULD OFFER A HAND WITH SHOPPING, TAKE THEM OUT, OR JUST STOP BY FOR A CHAT NOW AND THEN.

TOP TIPS TO HELP YOU CARE FOR OLDER PEOPLE

Here are some ideas:

1 MAKE A FAMILY STORY BOOK

Ask an older relative to tell you stories about your family and show you old photos. Then scan the photos, write down the stories, and turn it all into a Family Story Book! There's lots of software to help with projects like this. Your relative will be delighted, and it's a great way to understand your own history.

2 SHARING SKILLS

OLDER PEOPLE HAVE SKILLS TO SHARE, SUCH AS ART, COOKING, GARDENING, KNITTING AND SEWING ... ASK THEM TO TEACH YOU ONE. YOU'RE SKILLED TOO – SEE IF YOU CAN HELP THEM IF THEY HAVE ANY TECH PROBLEMS.

3 LISTEN

Perhaps they grew up in a different country and speak another language. Ask them all about it and learn some words! What did they do before they retired? Just listening with interest is a wonderful gift, but you can care in other ways too. Read them a story, or ask them to read one to you. Prepare a special meal together.

GOAL 6

UNDERSTANDING CULTURES

There are around **7.9 BILLION PEOPLE** living on the Earth today! And every single one of us is an individual in our own right. Part of what makes us all special are our cultures – our different foods, languages, clothes, arts, and beliefs.

This goal is a pretty big one. It's about caring for every single one of those 7.9 billion people by understanding and celebrating different cultures.

CELEBRATING different cultures:

REDUCES DISCRIMINATION AND RACISM.

CREATES A MORE BALANCED WORLD – WHEN WE APPRECIATE AND ENJOY THE DIFFERENCES IN PEOPLE, WE ALL MIX TOGETHER MORE HAPPILY.

Gives us other stories, ideas, and new ways of living.

Start by celebrating your own culture!

YOUR FAMILY MAY HAVE LIVED IN A PLACE FOR A LONG TIME, BUT YOU'LL STILL HAVE YOUR OWN FAMILY EXPRESSIONS, HOLIDAYS, CUSTOMS, AND FOOD. WHAT ARE THEY?

Maybe you came here from another country, with different traditions. Or perhaps your parents or grandparents did. Do you, or they, speak another language? Wear particular clothes? How do you celebrate special days?

Let's broaden our horizons and have fun by understanding our own cultures as well as those of others!

TOP TIPS FOR UNDERSTANDING CULTURES

Here's how to connect with and enjoy *all* our cultures!

MAKE A BOOK OR GIVE A PRESENTATION ABOUT YOUR CULTURE. IT MIGHT INCLUDE WORDS IN ANOTHER LANGUAGE, FAVORITE FOODS, AND DESCRIPTIONS OF SPECIAL OCCASIONS, OR RELIGIOUS STORIES AND FOLK TALES.

Ask your teacher about a class project to meet schoolchildren in different parts of the world.

VISIT DIFFERENT CULTURAL NEIGHBORHOODS AND COMMUNITIES IN YOUR OWN TOWN, DRINK IN THE ATMOSPHERE, AND SAMPLE SOME DELICIOUS FOOD. ART GALLERIES, MUSEUMS, BOOKS, AND FILMS ALSO TELL US ABOUT OTHER COUNTRIES AND CULTURES.

If you're lucky enough to have school friends from different cultures to your own, find out all about them.

Learn a new language. It helps you feel empathy for others – even if you only learn a few words.

PUT A WORLD MAP ON YOUR WALL, AND THEN PICK A COUNTRY. FIND OUT EVERYTHING YOU CAN ABOUT IT – YOU MIGHT GO THERE ONE DAY!

We all share the same world. Let's care for each other by understanding and interacting with people from all sorts of cultural backgrounds.

GOAL 7

CARING FOR ANIMALS

Did you know scientists have discovered that rabbits who are stroked lovingly every day are less likely to suffer heart disease than rabbits who aren't?

And that looking after a pet makes us feel capable, confident, happy, and increases our empathy?

IF YOU HAVE A PET AT HOME, YOU'LL KNOW THAT ANIMALS ARE INDIVIDUALS, JUST AS WE ARE. THEY CAN FEEL PAIN, HAPPINESS, LOVE, AND GRIEF, JUST LIKE US. DOGS EVEN SHOW EMPATHY – THEY CAN SENSE THEIR OWNER'S DISTRESS AND DO THEIR BEST TO CHEER THEM UP.

So let's be great friends back. And not just to our pets – but to ALL animals. That means making sure that farm animals live decent lives. And that all wild creatures – from the tiniest insect to the mightiest blue whale – are able to thrive in their chosen habitats.

CARING FOR ANIMALS MEANS LEARNING ABOUT THEM AND REALIZING THAT THEY ALL HAVE SPECIAL ROLES TO PLAY ON PLANET EARTH. LET'S SHOW THEM THE SAME KINDNESS WE SHOW OUR FRIENDS AND FAMILY.

TOP TIPS FOR CARING FOR ANIMALS

Whether we have a pet or not, we can still all care for animals.

If you do have a pet:

WRITE A LIST OF YOUR CURRENT PET RESPONSIBILITIES IN YOUR CARING NOTEBOOK. ADD ONE MORE RESPONSIBILITY AND MAKE SURE YOU STICK TO IT.

Each pet is different and has specific needs, so find out what's right for yours. There are some things that every animal needs to thrive: the right kind of food, plenty of fresh water, exercise, and a suitable place to sleep or to hide in. Most pets need grooming, too.

If you don’t have a pet:

Consider a rescue pet. Animal-rescue homes are full of animals, waiting for loving, forever homes.

VISIT A WILDLIFE CENTER, PETTING FARM, OR CITY FARM.

Many wildlife organizations allow you to “adopt” endangered animals. You could ask for this as a birthday gift. The money goes towards important conservation work.

LOOK FOR ANIMAL WELFARE LABELS ON MEAT, FISH, EGGS, MILK, CHEESE, AND OTHER DAIRY PRODUCTS. THIS MEANS THAT THESE FOODS CAME FROM FARM ANIMALS THAT ARE WELL LOOKED AFTER.

Caring for animals is one of the very kindest things you can do.

Go for it!

GOAL 8

CARING FOR PLANET EARTH

Our Earth is so precious. Its forests, mountains, oceans, lakes, and rivers form our environment, giving us fresh air to breathe, food to sustain us, and medicine to heal us.

We're part of it, along with all other living creatures. Without it, there would be no us. No wonder people call it Mother Earth.

BUT THE EARTH IS SUFFERING BECAUSE OF CLIMATE CHANGE AND THE LOSS OF HABITAT FOR WILD ANIMALS AND PLANTS.

One of the world's leading naturalists, **SIR DAVID ATTENBOROUGH**, says, *"If people lose knowledge, sympathy and understanding of the natural world, they're going to mistreat it."* We can make sure we care for the natural world by **GAINING KNOWLEDGE AND UNDERSTANDING** of the Earth.

Caring for nature is good for us!
Studies show that activities such as feeding birds, walking in the woods, and gardening lift our mood and make us feel calmer, happier, and healthier.
Who knew trash picking could be fun!
So, let's start at home! Do you have a garden? Or maybe you live near a park, woodland, or beach? Wherever you are, there are tons of ways that you can help care for planet Earth.

TOP TIPS FOR CARING FOR PLANET EARTH

Here's how we can make a real difference:

1 LEARN ABOUT NATURE

VISIT YOUR NEAREST NATURE RESERVE OR WILD PLACE AND FIND OUT ABOUT THE ANIMALS AND PLANTS THAT MAKE IT THEIR HOME.

2 JOIN A LITTER-COLLECTING GROUP IN YOUR AREA

If there isn't one, talk to friends and adults about starting one yourself. Whatever you can do will be really helpful.

3 HELP WILDLIFE AT HOME

PUT UP A NEST BOX FOR BIRDS, PROVIDE THEM WITH FOOD, AND MAKE SURE THEY HAVE FRESH WATER EVERY DAY. GROW INSECT-FRIENDLY FLOWERS IN YOUR GARDEN OR IN A CONTAINER OUTSIDE, OR MAKE A BUG HOTEL.

4 BECOME A CITIZEN SCIENTIST

Take part in surveys that count garden birds and small mammals, spot insects, and identify plants. These help care for the planet by giving us a bigger picture of how wildlife is changing and adapting to climate change and other pressures. Have a look on the internet to see what's going on near you.

5 GET *10 GREEN GOALS* OUT OF THE LIBRARY

IT TELLS YOU HOW YOU CAN HELP FIGHT THE CLIMATE CRISIS.

6 DO SOMETHING SPECIAL ON WORLD EARTH DAY

Talk to your teacher about this and get the whole school involved.

We've only got one Earth.
Let's care for it
as much as we can.

GOAL 9

MAKING UP

You've just had a big disagreement with your mom ... Or you forgot your friend's birthday and now they're ignoring you ... Or your little sister scribbled all over your homework and you've just yelled at her and made her cry ...

TAKE A DEEP BREATH AND TRY NOT TO WORRY. WE'RE ALL HUMAN AND WE ALL MAKE MISTAKES SOMETIMES. A VERY IMPORTANT PART OF CARING FOR PEOPLE IS MAKING UP – THAT MEANS SAYING SORRY IF WE'VE DONE OR SAID SOMETHING TO UPSET THEM AND TELLING THEM WHEN THEY'VE DONE OR SAID SOMETHING TO UPSET US.

Caring people are always sorry when they realize that they've hurt someone – and they'll do their best not to do it again.

HOLDING GRUDGES MEANS HOLDING NEGATIVE FEELINGS INSIDE THAT HARM US – NOT THE OTHER PERSON. SO, JUST AS IT'S NEVER TOO LATE TO SAY THANK YOU, IT'S NEVER TOO LATE TO MAKE UP.

And here's the good news – arguments aren't all bad! When we try to resolve them, we help strengthen friendships and problem-solving skills, and reveal the things that worry us. In this way, making up is part of caring for our nearest and dearest.

Life's too short to hold a grudge!

TOP TIPS FOR MAKING UP

There are always two sides to making up – saying sorry and accepting apologies. Here are some caring tips for both.

1 LISTEN

IF YOU HAVE A DISAGREEMENT, STAY QUIET AND LISTEN TO THE OTHER PERSON. DON'T INTERRUPT OR TELL THEM THEY'RE WRONG. TRY TO UNDERSTAND THEIR POINT OF VIEW.

2 APOLOGIZE

If you realize you've hurt someone, apologize and say why you're sorry. For example, "I'm sorry I said hurtful things to you." Sometimes you need to do something extra too, like replacing something you've broken.

3 STAY CALM

IF SOMEONE'S HURT YOU, TELL THEM WHEN YOU'RE FEELING CALM. RATHER THAN CRITICIZE THEM, LET THEM KNOW HOW THEIR ACTIONS OR WORDS MADE YOU FEEL. FOR EXAMPLE, "WHEN YOU FORGOT MY BIRTHDAY I FELT SAD AND THOUGHT YOU DIDN'T WANT TO BE MY FRIEND ANY MORE." A CARING FRIEND WILL APOLOGIZE AND WORK TO MAKE THINGS RIGHT.

Remember, if we practice it enough, kindness becomes a **positive habit!**

4 ACCEPT AND MOVE ON

Always accept an apology at once, then leave it behind you and move forward in a positive way. Perhaps now you understand that your mom was feeling tired when she shouted at you, or that your friend was sad when you forgot their birthday.

You've only just begun a lifetime full of caring and kindness. The caring habits you develop will grow and grow until they become second nature in **everything you do and say.**

GOAL 10

SAYING THANK YOU

How many times did you say thank you today? Did you thank the parent who prepared your food? The friend for saying they liked your new shoes? Your dog for welcoming you home with a wagging tail?

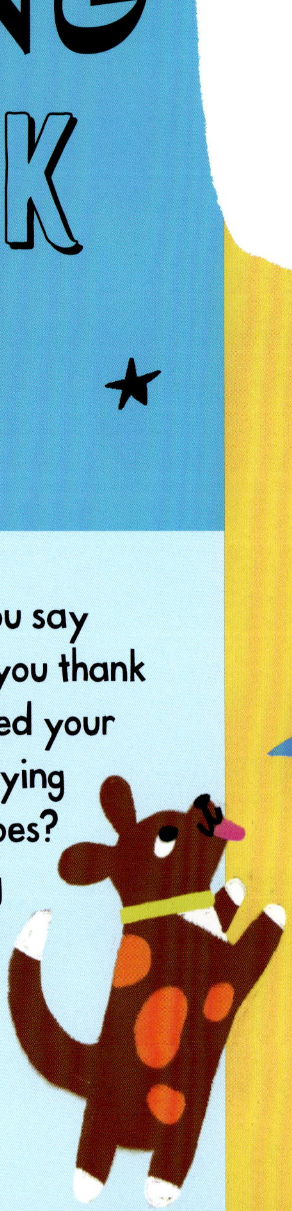

Saying thank you, or showing gratitude, is the flip side of being kind!

And it's just as important.

GRATITUDE MEANS REMEMBERING OTHER PEOPLE'S KINDNESS TO US AND CELEBRATING ALL THE GOOD THINGS WE HAVE. FEELING GRATEFUL MAKES US HAPPY. REMEMBER OXYTOCIN, THE FEEL-GOOD KINDNESS HORMONE? WE GET IT WHEN WE FEEL GRATITUDE AS WELL AS WHEN WE'RE KIND.

So from now on, say thank you to everyone who does anything to help you or make you feel happy. That means your friends, the people at home, AND all the others who care for us within our communities – such as teachers, nurses, doctors, and the carers who look after those of us who need extra help.

And remember, it's never too late to say thank you. So even if you didn't in the past – maybe you forgot to send a thank-you card – DO IT RIGHT NOW.

TOP TIPS FOR SAYING THANK YOU

Here are four great ways to feel and show your gratitude.

1 START A GRATITUDE SECTION

In your Caring Notebook, write a list of all the caring people you know and what they've done and said that's helped you. Have you said thank you to them? If not, make sure you do! Build up your gratitude and keep it going. Every day, write down two things that happened that you are thankful for.

2 THANK YOUR TEACHER

MAKE THEM A CARD SAYING HOW MUCH YOU APPRECIATE THEM.

3 SAY THANKS TO YOUR COMMUNITY

Give something back by asking your parent or carer about helping out at a food bank or a community garden. Donate used toys, books, and DVDs to hospitals, libraries, or daycare centers.

4 GRATITUDE MEDITATION

TRY THIS AS YOU GO ABOUT YOUR NORMAL DAY. AS YOU WALK AROUND THE HOUSE, THINK OF THE WORKERS WHO BUILT IT OR FIXED IT. AS YOU MAKE YOUR BED, THINK OF THE PEOPLE WHO PLANTED, PICKED, AND SPUN THE COTTON IN YOUR SHEETS. WHEN YOU EAT A BANANA, THINK OF THE PEOPLE WHO PLANTED AND TENDED THE TREE IT CAME FROM. WHEN WE USE THE PRODUCTS OF OTHER PEOPLE'S WORK, WE OWE THEM GRATITUDE.

GLOSSARY

APOLOGY – saying sorry for doing wrong.

BELIEF – the feeling of being certain that something exists or is true. It's often used to mean religious belief.

CLIMATE CHANGE – changes in the overall temperature of the Earth.

COMPASSION – the desire to help people or animals who are suffering.

CULTURE – a pattern of behavior, such as beliefs, arts, and traditions, that are shared by a group of people.

CUSTOM – a way of behaving, or a belief, that has existed for a long time.

DISCRIMINATION – when a person, or a group of people, are treated differently or unfairly.

EMPATHY – the ability to understand and share the emotions and feelings of another being.

ENDANGERED ANIMAL – an animal that is at risk of disappearing forever.

ENVIRONMENT – the air, water, and land where animals, people and plants live.

FORGIVENESS – not blaming someone or being angry with them for something they've said or done.

GRATITUDE – being aware of, and thankful for, the good things that happen to us.

HABITAT – the natural home of an animal or plant.

LANGUAGE – a form of communication by sounds, words, and grammar. There are over 7,000 languages spoken in the world!

NATURALIST – a person who studies or is an expert in plant or animals.

NATURE RESERVE – a protected area where plants and animals are left undisturbed.

OXYTOCIN – a hormone produced by the brain that's associated with happiness and partnership. It's sometimes called the "kindness hormone" or the "love hormone."

PROTEIN – a substance that builds, maintains, and replaces body tissues.

RACISM – a form of discrimination where people are treated unfairly because of their skin color or cultural background.

RELIGION – the belief in and worship of god or gods.

SELF-ESTEEM – the way you think and feel about yourself. Having good self-esteem means that you're mostly happy with the way you are.

STRESS – what you feel when you're worried or uncomfortable about something.

TOLERANCE – the acceptance of others, regardless of their behaviour or beliefs.

TRADITION – a belief or way of acting that a group of people have continued to follow for a long time.

FURTHER INFORMATION

WEBSITES:

childfun.com/recommendations/random-acts-of-kindness-for-kids/ – suggests 30 inspiring acts of kindness for kids!

ecofriendlykids.co.uk – a website for containing information to help explore the natural world and learn about environmental issues.

kids.nationalgeographic.com/science/article/green-tips – National Geographic Kids is full of great information about the natural world. This webpage gives tips about what we can do to help nature and lessen the impact of climate change.

redcross.org.uk/get-involved/teaching-resources/kindness-resource-list – lots of great activities and information about kindness, empathy and appreciating different cultures.

BOOKS:

Choose Kind Journal – Do One Wonderful Thing Every Day by R. J. Palacio, 2017, Penguin

Old Enough to Save the Planet by Loll Kirby, 2021, Magic Cat Publishing

The Good Guys – 50 Heroes Who Changed the World With Kindness by Rob Kemp and Paul Blow, 2018, Wren and Rook

We Are All Different by Tracey Turner, 2021, Kingfisher

INDEX